A New True Book

TYRANNOSAURUS REX

By David Petersen

CHILDRENS PRESS®

CHICAGO

Tyrannosaurus rex
(tih • RAN • oh • sore • uss REX)

PHOTO CREDITS

AP/Wide World Photos, Inc.—28 (left), 33

Art—Richard Wahl—11, 12 (top right & left), 37

American Museum of Natural History—
#PK212 (Cover), p. 5; #2423 p. 2;
#2827 p. 12 (left), 45; #2752 p. 17;
#2422 p. 18; #PK213 p. 19; #18342 p.
28 (right); #18172 p. 29; #18341 p.
31; #PK51 p. 36; #2421 p. 38 (top);
#2637 p. 38 (bottom); #324393 p. 44

Carnegie Museum of Natural History—
15, 35

Dinosaur National Monument/Shostal
Associates, Inc.—23

Used with permission from Dinosaur
Nature Association—39

Field Museum of Natural History—
#CK22T 78854 p. 4 (top)
#CK45T 73837 p. 4 (bottom)
#CK39T 66175 p. 6
#CK9T 59442 p. 21

DOUG LEE/Tom Stack & Associates—
43

Photo courtesy Museum of the
Rockies—25, 27

Yerkes Observatory Photograph—41
(both)

Cover: Tyrannosaurus rex drawing by
Charles Knight

Library of Congress Cataloging-in-Publication Data

Petersen, David.
    Tyrannosaurus Rex / by David Petersen.
        p.   cm.—(A New true book)
    Includes index.
    Summary: Describes the possible appearance and
behavior of this large dinosaur and the fossil
discoveries providing this information.
    ISBN 0-516-01167-7
    1.   Tyrannosaurus rex—Juvenile literature.
[1.   Tyrannosaurus rex.   2.   Dinosaurs.
3.   Paleontology.]   I.   Title.
QE862.S3P48   1989   88-38054
567.3'7—dc19   CIP
                                      AC

TABLE OF CONTENTS

Above: The lizard-shaped Casea and the meat-eating,
fin-back Dimetrodon (dih • MEH • trah • don) were prehistoric animals.
Below: Prehistoric meat-eating reptiles, Cynognathus (sin • NAWG • nah • thus),
close in on a defenseless Kannemeyeria (kah • nih • my • AIR • ee • ya).

KING OF THE TYRANT DINOSAURS

In a time long before the first people, great beasts ruled the Earth. Because many of these beasts looked like giant lizards, scientists named them "dinosaurs." This name comes from two Greek words: *deinos*, meaning terrible or monstrous, and *sauros*, meaning lizard. Thus, dinosaur means "terrible lizard."

Archaeopteryx (ar • kay • OP • ter • ix) was a flying dinosaur. Compsognathus (cahmp • SAWG • na • thus) was a very small dinosaur that walked on two legs.

However, not all dinosaurs were monstrous and frightening. Some dinosaurs were no larger than chickens. Others were bigger than train cars, but they were gentle. They ate only plants.

Yet, one group of dinosaurs were very big and very frightening. They were the "theropods," meat-eating dinosaurs that walked on two legs.

The fiercest theropod was *Tyrannosaurus rex*.

"Tyrannosaurus" comes from the Greek words *tyrannos*, meaning tyrant, and *sauros*, meaning lizard. "Rex" is the Latin word for king. Thus, Tyrannosaurus rex means

Tyrannosaurus rex was a meat eater.

"king of the tyrant lizards."
Tyrannosaurus rex was a
true monster. It was about
forty feet long and
weighed over seven tons, or
fourteen thousand pounds.

Tyrannosaurus was heavier than two large elephants.

Oddly, Tyrannosaurus had relatively tiny arms. They were less than three feet long and couldn't even reach its mouth.

What use were these small arms to Tyrannosaurus? Some scientists believe they were used not for grasping or eating, but for raising itself up off the ground after a rest.

Each "hand" had two long claws. The claws could have been used to dig into the ground to keep its heavy body from sliding when raising itself.

Unlike its arms, Tyrannosaurus rex's legs were huge. Imagine an animal with legs ten feet long. An adult human standing next to the leg would barely reach its *knees*.

TYRANNOSAURUS REX

The skeleton of
Tyrannosaurus rex (left).
The drawing (above) compares
the size of Tyrannosaurus rex
with a modern horse.

Tyrannosaurus needed
its long, strong legs to
support its big body. This
giant stood almost twenty
feet tall. That means it
easily could have peeked
into a second-story window.

Scientists once thought Tyrannosaurus rex walked almost upright and dragged a very long tail behind. Most drawings and museum displays show it standing and walking this way.

Recently, however, some scientists have come to believe the creature may have walked leaning forward with its back almost parallel to the ground. The tail, they think, was short and fat. It was carried off the ground. This way, the tail would balance the weight of the huge head and allow Tyrannosaurus to move quickly.

Tyrannosaurus rex may have been fast, but it probably wasn't graceful. By studying the bones of its legs and feet, scientists have learned that Tyrannosaurus probably was pigeon-toed. When Tyrannosaurus walked, its

Tyrannosaurus rex skeleton

stubby tail would have
swung heavily from side to
side, making the tyrant
king waddle like a duck.
    Each foot had sharp
claws eight inches long.

15

These claws probably were used to hold other animals. Tyrannosaurus held its victims and killed them with its terrible teeth. Its four-foot jaws worked like scissors.

Each tooth was up to six inches long, curved, jagged, and thick. With

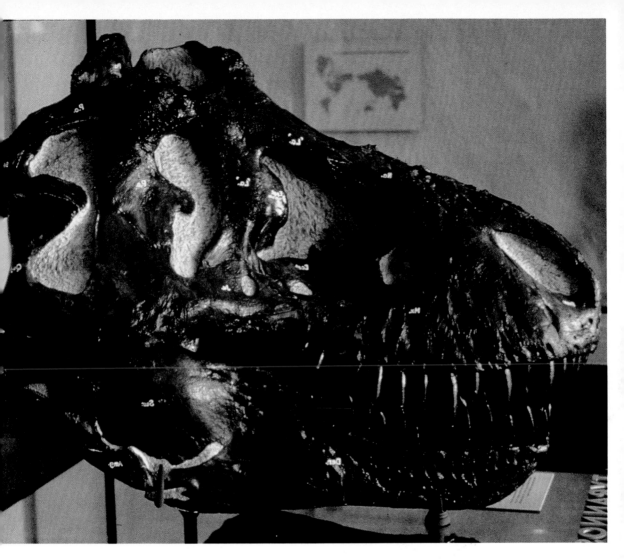

such teeth, the big hunter
and scavenger easily
could rip huge chunks of
flesh from other dinosaurs.

Hadrosaur (HAD • droh • sore)

One dinosaur that Tyrannosaurus hunted was the *hadrosaur*. These animals also are called duck-billed dinosaurs, because of the shapes of their heads. They were vegetarians and had no means of defending themselves.

Another of Tyrannosaurus's victims was large and dangerous. This was *Triceratops*—a 25-foot-long, three-horned vegetarian.

Triceratops

DEATH AND BURIAL

Let's travel back in time 70 million years, to a time scientists call the *Cretaceous* period. Imagine that you see a herd of Triceratops feeding near a river.

Suddenly, from behind a nearby hill, appears the big, toothy head of Tyrannosaurus. The river blocks the Triceratops'

Battle between Triceratops and Tyrannosaurus rex

escape, and Tyrannosaurus attacks one.

Desperately, Triceratops fights back by thrusting its three pointed horns into its attacker's belly.

Let's pretend that the two dinosaurs killed each other in the fight, near the river.

Perhaps both were killed by a landslide, flood, or other natural disaster. Or maybe they just happened to die near the ancient river at different times.

Eventually, their flesh decayed or was eaten by scavengers, leaving only two huge skeletons. Floods washed the bones into the river where they were covered by sand and silt.

During the years that followed, the dinosaur

bones eventually rotted
and dissolved bit by bit.
Minerals in the water
replaced each bit until
only the minerals remained
as perfect casts.
Mineralized bones are one
kind of "fossil."

North wall of the quarry at Dinosaur National Monument

The river eventually changed course or dried up. The fossilized dinosaur bones lay buried in the ground for millions of years. Then, natural forces within the Earth pushed the ground and the buried bones up.

In time the earth above the bones was worn away or "eroded," by wind and rain. Finally, some of the fossilized bones could be seen on the side of the hill.

FINDING DINOSAUR FOSSILS

One day in 1901, at a place now called Hell Creek, Montana, a hunter was crossing an eroded hillside when he spotted a mound of large, fossilized bones.

Hell Creek, Montana

The old bones interested
the hunter, who was also
a scientist.

One bone was
particularly odd. It was
long and pointed, like the
tip of a giant horn. The
hunter saved the bone to
take home to New York.

Another member of a
hunting party, who was
also a scientist, took
pictures of the hill.

In New York the two
hunters showed the fossil

Excavation of a Triceratops bone

bone and pictures to "paleontologists," scientists who study fossils.

One paleontologist who saw the pointed bone was Barnum Brown of the American Museum of Natural History. Brown

Dr. Barnum Brown (left) of the American Museum of Natural History discovered and photographed this Triceratops skull (right).

identified the fossil as a horn from the dinosaur Triceratops. This was exciting news.

In the summer of 1902, Barnum Brown and two other scientists traveled to Montana to search for fossils. At Hell Creek, they

Dr. Brown and his team work on the excavation in 1905.

found more bones from Triceratops. Nearby, they also found some much larger bones. They had never seen bones like this before.

Using dynamite, plows, and pickaxes, the scientists began to unearth their mysterious find.

Later, these new bones were identified as belonging to the largest flesh-eating animal ever to walk the Earth—Tyrannosaurus rex, king of the tyrant lizards.

The heaviest fossil bone found was a hip bone. It weighed more than a pickup truck.

After digging for two years, Barnum Brown decided he had found all the remaining bones of

A huge hip bone is removed from the site.

this strange "new"
dinosaur that had lived 70
million years ago.

Workers loaded the
bones onto train cars for
the trip back to New York.

At the American
Museum, in 1904, Barnum

Brown and other scientists began cleaning, identifying, and preserving the bones. As they worked, they discovered that some parts of the Tyrannosaurus skeleton were missing.

In 1908, Barnum Brown found the bones of a second Tyrannosaurus. These bones also were shipped to the museum and were used to help piece together the first skeleton.

Skeleton of Tyrannosaurs rex (left) towers over students making molds of the smaller Triceratops at the American Museum of Natural History in New York City.

But even with two partial skeletons, there were some missing bones. For these, the scientists estimated the original size and shape, then molded substitutes from plaster.

Finally, after many years' work, the first complete skeleton of Tyrannosaurus rex was put together. This skeleton still stands in New York City's American Museum of Natural History.

Later, the second Tyrannosaurus skeleton was restored and sent to the Carnegie Museum of Natural History in Pittsburgh, Pennsylvania. It can be viewed there today.

Opposite page: Tyrannosaurus rex skeleton at the Carnegie Museum of Natural History

The first dinosaur eggs ever found are displayed at the American Museum of Natural History.

THE GREAT DYING

The dinosaurs appeared about 200 million years ago.

Like lizards and snakes, the dinosaurs laid eggs. Yet, they probably were

not cold-blooded reptiles.
But they were not
mammals, like people,
horses, and elephants. The
dinosaurs were warm-
blooded animals.

Tyrannosaurus rex (left) had lizardlike
hip bones. Other dinosaurs (right) had hip
bones much like a modern bird.

Lizardlike
hip bones

Birdlike
hip bones

The dinosaurs ruled the
Earth for millions of years.
They were one of the most
successful forms of land
animal ever to live.

Why, then, some 65 million years ago, did all the dinosaurs disappear?

No one knows exactly, but there are several theories to account for the dinosaurs' extinction. One theory involves an asteroid impact. This would have happened when an asteroid, meteor, or "shooting star" hit the Earth.

The resulting explosion could have created clouds

Comet Morehouse (left) photographed in 1908. The Barringer Meteor Crater near Winslow, Arizona was made when a meteor hit Earth about 20,000 or 40,000 years ago. This crater is 600 feet deep and nearly one mile across.

of dust that might have blotted out the sun for many years.

Days would have become as dark as nights. Temperatures would have dropped lower and lower. Without sunlight and warmth, plants could no longer live.

With the trees and
shrubs gone, the plant-
eating dinosaurs soon
would have died out.
Without the plant eaters to
feed on, Tyrannosaurus rex
and the other meat eaters
would have starved to
death.

Maybe it happened that
way. Maybe not.

Another theory suggests
that the dinosaurs
disappeared gradually. As

Park City Formation, Split Mountain Campground
at Dinosaur National Monument in Utah

the Earth's climate slowly
became colder and dryer,
the dinosaurs could not
adapt and died.

43

Dinosaur
footprints

Either way, the giant
dinosaurs are gone. All
that remains are their
fossilized bones, eggs,
footprints, and close
relatives—birds.

However, for longer than any of us can imagine, dinosaurs ruled the Earth. King of them all was Tyrannosaurus rex.

WORDS YOU SHOULD KNOW

asteroid(AST • er • roid) — one of a group of objects that are smaller than planets and that orbit the Sun between Mars and Jupiter

cold-blooded(KOHLD BLUH • ded) — having a body temperature that is about the same as that of the surroundings; warm in the sun and cool in the shade

Cretaceous(kreh • TAY • shuss) — a period of Earth's history that lasted from 130 million to 65 million years ago

dinosaur(DYNE • uh • sore) — any of a group of extinct animals that dominated the earth many millions of years ago; some grew to enormous size

estimated(ESS • tih • may • tid) — made a guess based on known measurements

extinction(ex • TINK • shun) — the dying out of a species of plant or animal

fossilized(FAWSS • ihl • ized) — turned into a fossil, the hardened remains of a plant or animal that lived long ago

graceful(GRAISS • ful) — moving with ease and smoothness

hadrosaur(HAD • roh • sore) — one of a group of large plant-eating dinosaurs that had large heads with ducklike bills

mammal(MAM • el) — one of a group of warm-blooded animals that have hair and nurse their young with milk

monstrous(MON • struss) — like a monster; huge

paleontologist(pail • ee • en • TAHL • ih • jist) — a scientist who studies the fossil remains of life from past periods of the Earth's history

parallel(PAIR • uh • lel) — on lines the same distance apart and going in the same direction, as railroad tracks

pigeon-toed(PIH • jin TOHD) — walking with the toes turned in

preserving(prih • ZER • ving) — saving from decay or wear

scavenger(SKAV • en • jir) — an animal that eats other animals that are found dead, rather than killing its prey

theropod(THAIR • uh • pahd) — a group of meat-eating dinosaurs that had small front legs and that walked on their very large hind legs

Triceratops(try • SAIR • uh • tops) — a large plant-eating dinosaur with three horns and a large bony hood or crest on its head

tyrant(TY • rent) — a harsh ruler who has complete power and who is often cruel and unjust

vegetarian(vej • ih • TAIR • ee • en) — an animal that eats only plants

warm-blooded(WARM BLUH • ded) — having a body temperature that is controlled from inside the body and is not dependent on the outside temperature

INDEX

About the Author

David Petersen is a senior editor for Mother Earth News *magazine,
and author of* Among the Elk *(Northland Publishing Company, 1988).
He has written eight titles in the True Book series.*